MALACHY DOYLE

Robin Hood
and the
Golden Arrow

Illustrated by
Martin Ursell

OXFORD
UNIVERSITY PRESS

OXFORD

UNIVERSITY PRESS

Great Clarendon Street, Oxford OX2 6DP

Oxford University Press is a department of the University of Oxford.
It furthers the University's objective of excellence in research, scholarship,
and education by publishing worldwide in

Oxford New York

Athens Auckland Bangkok Bogotá Buenos Aires Calcutta
Cape Town Chennai Dar es Salaam Delhi Florence Hong Kong Istanbul
Karachi Kuala Lumpur Madrid Melbourne Mexico City Mumbai
Nairobi Paris São Paulo Shanghai Singapore Taipei Tokyo Toronto Warsaw

and associated companies in Berlin Ibadan

Oxford is a trade mark of Oxford University Press
in the UK and in certain other countries

Text © Malachy Doyle 2001
The moral rights of the author have been asserted
Database right Oxford University Press (maker)
First published 2001

British Library Cataloguing in Publication Data
Data available

ISBN 0 19 917424 5

Printed in Hong Kong

Available in packs

Year 3 / Primary 4 Pack of Six (one of each book) ISBN 0 19 917427 X
Year 3 / Primary 4 Class Pack (six of each book) ISBN 0 19 917428 8

Contents

1

The Sheriff's Revenge

"I'm going to catch that Robin Hood, if it's the last thing I do! Stealing from the rich to give to the poor, indeed! I've had enough of it!"

The Sheriff of Nottingham was furious. He'd been outwitted by Robin and his band of merry outlaws once too often.

Day after day it happened – the

nasty Sheriff would get up in the morning, looking forward to throwing some poor unfortunate family out of their home because they couldn't pay their rent, only to arrive at their cottage to find them sitting round the table with a slap-up meal in front of them and a large bag of money to pay him with.

And where had they got all that food and money, all of a sudden, the Sheriff asked them, when the last time he'd seen them they hadn't two pennies to rub together? They wouldn't tell him, of course, but he knew, all right. Robin Hood, that's where!

And where had Robin Hood got the money? The Sheriff of Nottingham knew the answer to

that one too. He stole it! Stole it
from the rich, who couldn't take a
ride in their coaches, couldn't even
set foot out of their houses any more
for fear of being ambushed by Robin

Hood and his bunch of unruly troublemakers.

Day after day the Sheriff and his men set off into Sherwood Forest to capture them, and day after day they returned, empty-handed.

Night after night the Sheriff lay awake, his poor tired brain clicking and whirring, full of thoughts of how the outlaw leader was making him look stupid in front of his own people, and of how to get his revenge on Robin.

"I must catch him! I will catch him!" cried the Sheriff, tossing and turning. But there was no way round it – whatever he planned, whatever he did, it never worked. Robin was just too clever for him.

Suddenly, at last, the Sheriff had a brainwave. He'd call a contest! A contest to decide who was the best bowman in England! Robin would be bound to enter, and then, once and for all, his arch-rival would be at his mercy.

"Fetch me my manservant!" the Sheriff cried to the guard at the door. And, although it was the middle of the night, his trusty servant had to come and listen to his master's plans.

"Spread the word far and wide," the Sheriff ordered, when he had told him what he had in mind. "And make sure it reaches Sherwood Forest. I want to be certain that villain, Robin Hood, hears all about it!"

"Sorry I'm late," cried Will Scarlet the following day, catching his breath. "I've been in town. Have you heard the news?"

The rest of Robin's company were already assembled under The Great Oak in the middle of Sherwood Forest, where they gathered each evening.

"What news is that, Will?" asked Robin. Most of his gang steered clear of the town for fear of being recognized by the Sheriff's men, but Will Scarlet was a master of disguise, so it was safer for him.

"There's to be an archery contest in the grounds of the castle," replied Will. "The winner is to receive a golden arrow!"

"A golden arrow?" said Little

John, with a great booming laugh. "Why would anyone want a golden arrow?"

"They say it's worth a small fortune," said Will. "The shaft is made of silver, and the head and feathers are pure gold."

"What do I care for gold and silver?" said Robin, spotting a leaf falling from a tree and raising his bow. In an instant, he let loose an arrow, which flashed through the air and impaled the falling leaf, pinning it to the trunk, inches above the head of Friar Tuck.

"Sorry, Friar," said Robin, helping the shaken monk back to his feet. "I just wanted to prove a point. But if the Sheriff of Nottingham wants to entice me out into the open, he'll

have to think up a better plan than that!"

He was a proud man, however, and the sly Sheriff knew it. It was not enough for Robin to be a hero to the common people. Not enough to be the leader of the bravest men in England. Robin was the finest archer in the land, without a doubt, and this was his chance to prove it.

So after a day of hunting and a day of thinking, he called his men together.

"Will Scarlet," he said, "I want you to find me your best disguise, so that I can enter this contest."

"But Robin," cried Little John, "you'll be walking into a trap! For even if the Sheriff doesn't recognize you, he'll know who you are when he sees your skill with the bow."

"Don't worry, John," said Robin. "I shall not be on my own. Each of you, my brave men, will be with me, mingling with the crowds. If the Sheriff tries to capture me, I know I can rely on you to get me out of trouble."

2

England's Finest

And so it was, on the day of the great contest, that the meadow below the Castle of Nottingham was ablaze with excitement. Flags of every colour fluttered in the breeze, and everyone from miles around had gathered to watch.

The Sheriff's men were under strict instructions to keep an eye out

for Robin's outlaws, and to capture
any that they spotted. But Will
Scarlet, the master of disguise, had
done well. Dressed as peasants,
tinkers, beggars and merchants, with
their weapons well hidden beneath

their cloaks, not one of them could
be recognized.

The Sheriff stepped forward,
holding up The Golden Arrow. As
the sunlight flashed on its silver
shaft, the people fell silent.

"Who has come to claim this magnificent prize?" he proclaimed, and twenty-four of the finest bowmen in England stood up from their places in the crowd and raised their bows above their heads.

"Step forward, men," said the Sheriff, beckoning them towards him. He examined each one carefully as they approached him, but failed to spot his rival, Robin Hood. At first he was disappointed, for he had dearly wished to lay hands on his enemy in front of such a crowd, and show the people that it was he, the mighty Sheriff of Nottingham, who was in control.

But as the archers prepared for the contest, stringing their bows tightly, selecting their best arrows, the Sheriff thought of a way to turn things to his advantage.

"I see that the one they call Robin Hood is not among you, my fine bowmen!" he cried, loudly so that everyone in the crowd

might also hear. "It does not surprise me, for I have always known him to be a coward as well as a rogue. I knew he would not dare to show his face in my presence!"

A murmur went through the crowd then, for Robin was their hero. Times were hard, the laws were harsh, and the poor people of England were very grateful to Robin for the many ways in which he helped them. Who else would bring food to the hungry, and money to those who could not afford to pay their rents? Who else but Robin Hood and his band of fearless warriors would dare to challenge the cruelty of the evil Sheriff?

The people who had come to watch the contest that day were

poor, yes, but they were not simple
folk. They all knew that the Sheriff
had set a trap for Robin, but their
faith in their hero was great. They
knew that Robin's pride would bring
him to the contest, but hoped
beyond hope that he would find a
way to outsmart the cruel Sheriff
once more. And it would give them
great joy to be there to see it.

3

Let the Contest Begin!

"Let the contest begin!" cried the
Sheriff, and a great cheer rang out
across the meadow. Then, as the
crowd settled down, the first
competitor stepped forward, raised
his bow and prepared to shoot.

The targets were willow
branches, pushed firmly into the

ground. It took great skill to hit the slender branch from such a distance, but even more to split it down the middle.

After each bowman had fired his first shot, the broken willows were replaced and the men took a step

back, preparing to fire again. Gradually, gradually, they moved further and further down the field, away from their targets, until only the very best of them could still split the willow with every shot they fired. One miss, and they had to withdraw into the crowd, bowing their heads in defeat.

In time it was clear that four of the archers stood head and shoulders above the rest. All four had managed to split the willow with every single shot, and the Sheriff beckoned them towards him.

"Call out your names, o mighty bowmen!" he cried, holding up the prize. "For before this day is done, one of you will be the proud owner of this golden arrow."

"My name is Adam the Red," announced the first, "and I am the finest archer in Nottingham!" And the Sheriff smiled a sly smile, for Adam was his own, his head bowman. If the Sheriff was not going to capture Robin Hood that day, then his plan was to at least do everything within his power to make sure that Adam won the competition. That way, hopefully the people would begin to give him the respect he felt he deserved.

"And I am Cruikshank of

Tamworth!" roared the second, pushing Adam out of the way. "I have travelled many miles to be here, for I am, without doubt, the finest bowman in England!"

"William of Cornwall!" bellowed the third, elbowing his way forward. "And I have travelled further, much further than any one of you. Word of this contest, my good Sheriff, has spread to all the corners of the land, and I have come here today to show you my stupendous skills. For I am, indeed, the greatest archer in all the world!"

After all this fine boasting, the eyes of the crowd turned then to the fourth bowman, who seemed quite happy to remain hidden behind the others. What could he say to better

that, they wondered? But he stayed
silent.

"What is your name, man?" the
Sheriff demanded, annoyed at his
silence. But the archer did not
answer.

"Tell me your name!" the Sheriff
cried, but yet again there was no

response. The silent bowman pointed to his mouth, shaking his head, and the Sheriff's manservant whispered something in his master's ear.

"Aha," said the Sheriff, a look of understanding crossing his face at last. "You cannot speak! Well let us hope that your bow works better than your tongue, my good man!" And he looked up, expecting the crowd to laugh heartily at his joke. But they did not.

"Silent Brown, we shall call you," said the Sheriff, for the archer was dressed in the clothes of a peasant, brown from tip to toe. A hood covered his head, and his face, beneath, was dark with wood ash.

A murmur went through the

crowd, then a whispering of another, more famous name. A name that led the people to nod, and point, and smile. But the Sheriff was too puffed up to notice the mood of the crowd, too pleased with himself to think that things might turn against him.

4

The Trembling Willow

The willows were replaced once
more, and each of the four
remaining competitors were led to
the position from which they must
fire. This time they were taken to a
point not one, but a full ten paces
behind the previous line.

At one end of the field stood four

mighty archers, at the other end
stood four thin sticks of willow, and
all around were the people of
Nottingham, holding their breath.

"Get ready!" cried the Sheriff,
and the archers raised their bows

and placed their arrows.

"Take aim!" cried the Sheriff, and each man pulled back the bow to its fullest extent. "And fire!"

Four arrows streaked through the air and each one found its way, sure and true, to the heart of the willow. There was a great roar of applause from the crowd, for never before had such skill, such keen competition, been seen in the grounds of the Castle of Nottingham.

Another ten steps back and another four sticks of willow. Another hush descended on the crowd and another swoop of arrows. But this time two of them glanced off the target, falling to the ground, and there was a gasp of disappointment.

Cruikshank and William turned away shamefaced, for their high hopes and proud boasts had come to nothing. They slunk off, into the crowd, and a great cheer arose as

the remaining two were called by the Sheriff. "Step forward, Adam the Red!" he cried. "Step forward, Silent Brown. For today one of you shall indeed be proved the finest bowman in England!"

"And it had better be you," he whispered into the ear of Adam, as he went past. "Or you're finished!"

And so there were two. They were each to fire three arrows, at three separate rods, from four hundred paces.

Twice, Adam the Red shot dead centre, splitting each willow stake cleanly, and each time his efforts were greeted with a mighty cheer from the Sheriff and his men. His third arrow hit the willow once more, but it was slightly off-centre. It scraped the slippery wood without cracking it and fell to the ground.

A look of alarm crossed the face of the Sheriff, but he quickly regained control.

"Excellent!" he cried, clapping his bowman on the shoulder. Then he whispered something to his manservant, who went running down to the other end of the meadow, where the rods were being replaced.

The Sheriff turned to the final competitor. "You may resign if you wish, Silent Brown," he said, "before you make a fool of yourself, for I do not see how you can possibly win. To do so, you must split all three willow rods, and from this distance surely that is impossible!"

But the peasant stepped forward, and the people held their breath as he pulled an arrow from his quiver. Quickly, he drew his bow, firing straight and true.

As the arrow hit the willow with a sharp crack, the stranger was already reloading his bow. The

second rod was also split, but as he
went to fire his third arrow a slight
breeze blew from the east and the
last willow was seen to waver. It had
not been pushed firmly enough into
the ground!

The unknown bowman heard a
strangled laugh from
beside him, and
turned to see an
evil smile on
the face of
the Sheriff.
It was a
trick!

The Sheriff was determined to see him lose, determined to see his own man win!

The silent archer was unable to complain. He had no voice, and therefore no choice. No choice but to wait for things to turn again in his favour, no choice but to wait for the wind to settle.

"Hurry up, man!" cried the Sheriff, but the bowman took his time. And then, when he detected that the wind had dropped enough for his arrow to fly sure and true, the archer took aim and fired. His arrow shot through the air, straight to the very heart of the willow, splitting it in two. A mighty cheer arose from the people watching, and in order to prove that he was indeed

the greatest of all bowmen, Robin
fired a fourth arrow. With a sharp
crack it split the previous one, right
down the middle, sending feathers
fluttering to the ground.

5

Three Cheers for Robin!

"This belongs to me!" cried Robin, tossing aside his hood. He grasped the golden arrow from the hands of the Sheriff and ran into the cheering crowd.

"It's Robin Hood!" gasped the Sheriff, recognizing him at last. "Arrest that man!"

The Sheriff's men drew their swords and rushed towards him, but they were too late. For the crowd, delighted that Robin had got the better of the wicked Sheriff once more, had rushed onto the field, surrounding their hero, so that in a matter of seconds he was hidden completely.

All of Robin's men kept watch to
make sure that their leader was safe
from the Sheriff's guards and Little
John, dressed as a beggar, pushed his
way through the people and
wrapped a green cloak around

Robin's shoulders, to disguise him once more.

And so it was that the Sheriff of Nottingham was left standing in the middle of the field, shaking with fury, as Robin slipped away unnoticed.

"Three cheers for Robin Hood, the champion bowman of all England!" cried Maid Marian, Robin's admirer, who had managed to slip away from Nottingham Castle and join her many friends.

"And now, let the music begin!" Maid Marian took the golden arrow from Robin's hand, laid it on a tree stump, and led him in a dance.

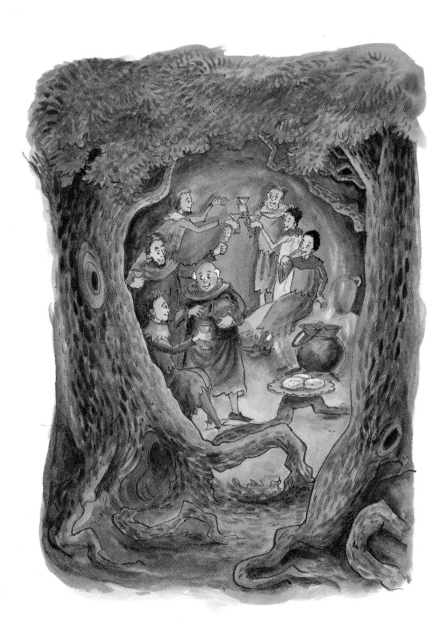

The celebrations, under The Great Oak in The Forest of Sherwood, lasted all that night and well into the next day. There was singing and dancing, eating and drinking, laughing and joking. Will Scarlet was congratulated for his skill at disguise, Little John and the others for helping Robin to escape, but the hero of the hour, as always, was Robin himself.

And the joke, as ever, was on the Sheriff of Nottingham, the evil Sheriff of Nottingham, who had tried to trick Robin Hood, but who had met his match once more.

About the author

I didn't realize I was an author until I was forty. Now I'm making up for lost time by writing every day, unless I'm out visiting schools or walking in the mountains. Most of my ideas come from inside my head but sometimes they start from stories I knew when I was a child. I used to play Robin Hood games with my big brother, Raphael. I always wanted to be Robin but somehow I always ended up as the evil Sheriff of Nottingham.